A brief

I have two younger brothers, Denny, who is just over 3 years younger than I, and Scott, who is just over 5 years younger. We grew up in Ann Arbor, Michigan. Our parents were very family-oriented. We always had a parent home. Mom didn't go back to work until Scott was in junior high, I think, and even then, she went to work at 4, after our dad came home. And we spent a lot of time with our aunts, uncles and cousins.

Because I was a product of our dad's first marriage (my birthmother died soon after I was born), I had an extra set of aunts, uncles and cousins. Our parents made sure I got to spend time with them as well.

Our dad was an athlete so my brothers and I grew up participating in sports. We played baseball in the neighborhood and later, my brothers played in school and as young adults, they coached a women's baseball team.. We ice skated, rode bikes, played golf, bowled and skied. We played marbles and and flew kites. We also learned to love watching sports, especially football.

Our mom was a homemaker and played games with us and did art projects. She taught us our manners and to take good care of our possessions. When she went back to work, she worked the 4pm to 10pm shift so that she could greet my dad after he got off work and turn us three over to him. She always had dinner prepared so he had minimal cooking to do for dinner. She did all the shopping while Dad sat in the car and read the paper. She didn't drive and my recollection is because she once hit the gas instead of the brake and ran into the back of the garage. And I didn't know until after college that she sewed her clothes before she was married and was quite accomplished at it.

Our dad's company, Argus Cameras, had a private access area at a nearby lake, Independence Lake, and in summers, we would picnic there and Mom would make an awesome picnics for us. We swam, caught frogs, and played in the woods. We also had lots of picnics in our backyard and in the winter, Dad would make an ice rink there for us. He would also go out into the rural areas and shovel sand into the trunk of the car for a sandbox for us to play in when we were little.

Every summer Dad would take off the last two weeks of July and we'd go stay in a cabin somewhere. Mom packed everything for all of us, including boxes of activities she would create for each of us to keep us entertained in the car driving on our vacations. We stayed in all the best locations of Michigan: Houghton Lake, Traverse City, Grand and South Haven, and Ludington. On one of my returns to Michigan with my husband, I took him to see some of the Lake Michigan beaches and he was quite awe-stricken as he had no idea we had such big, beautiful beaches.

When I graduated from high school, I went to Eastern Michigan University and a year later transferred to the University of Michigan and graduated from there. I fulfilled a dream I'd had since 3rd grade by moving to Hawai'i. I was a waitress, a teacher, a therapist and a homeschooling mom. Denny went to Eastern for his degree and and became a history teacher, beloved by students, parents and faculty alike. Scott graduated from Washtenaw Community College and became a beat cop everyone liked and later he was in charge of the fitness program at a low security prison. My brothers bought condos in the same complex as our parents so they were always there to help one another out.

Both brothers enjoyed traveling and treated our parents to many trips, even Ireland twice. Las Vegas was their favorite and even now, Denny loves to go down the a casino and everyone knows and appreciates him. He had a fierce battle with cancer and won.   Scott and I are more the exercise fanatics and a bit the health nuts when it comes to diets

I met my husband, Jordan, a Maui native, in Honolulum and we have a son, also named Jordan but we nickname him Thumper before he was born. The folks called him JP and he goes by his given name, Jordan, in his cinematography business, HiFocused.com. We have visited our Michigan family at least every other year and Scott visited us once. Jordan and I hope to get both brothers out here to visit at least one more time.

Scottisms

This book actually originated with my writing down the unique ways Scott would describe things. I had never heard most of them so I just started jotting them down with no idea what I'd do with them.

Doesn't know s*** from Shinola (Shinola was a tyle of shoe polish)

You can play hardball but you'd better bring the juice

He'd complain if you hung him with a new rope

The okie dokie was thrown down (deception)

All that and a bag of chips

Needle is stuck on stupid

Double down on stupid

He's got long paper (plenty of money)

Like a can of corn (catch was easy)

Gets a fur ball (about something)

Hold the roll

Sitting on ready

She's got big grapefruit (She's not going to take any crap)

Get in the trunk (When somcone's talking crazy)

Wound up like an 8 day clock

Same god, different pew

I've got it; you take it (fielding a fly ball)

They'll spit the bit. (Do well until they face a good team)

Recipes

Scott has always had a quirky way of eating. He makes his menus and then follows them religiously and at exact times. His menus have limited items but he really enjoys what he does eat.

Note:
* Apples are always Honeycrisp or Cosmic Crisp.
* Bread is always Ezekial, low sodium,
       preferable 7 Sprouted Grain.
* Yoghurt is Greek non-fat and Kefir is (Lifeway).
* Protein bars are Pure Protein brand, preferably
       double chocolate flavor

Scott's Potpourri

Apple cut in bite size pieces, skin on. Add about equal amounts of raw peanuts, frozen peas, and a small box of Sun Valley Raisin (size just smaller than a deck of cards). You could add a dressing but no need.

Nutty Apple

Unpeeled small apple sliced thin. Spread each slice with Maranatha nut butter, peanut or almond no salt, no sugar

Fur ball (named by Jordan and some neighborhood men when they all went fishing in AK) Wet 2 pieces bread & make snowball out of it. Microwave & eat. It tastes like stuffing.

Apple Omlet

2 eggs mixed and put in one side of a microwave-safe omlet maker. Cover with thinly sliced apples, enough to cover the egg. Sprinkle with ground cinammon. Close omlet maker and cook for about 1:15. Experiment to see how much time it takes to cook the eggs the way you like them. About a minute and 15 seconds.

Sloppy protein

Two slices bread, on plate and pour water over them until soaked and pour off excess water.. Microwave for 70-75 seconds, pour off excess water and cover with Muscle Double Knock-Out 32 gram protein. Eat with a fork like French Toast.

Sloppy Protein Double Down

Two slices bread with protein bar cut in 9 pieces and put on top. Rinse water over it & wet until it's pretty wet and microwave for 88 seconds.

Scott's finger tap eggs

Mix 2 jumbo eggs and a heaping silver tablespoon of yogurt. Don't worry if it's a little lumpy. Place in one half of a microwavable omlet maker. Cut up a protein bar into 9 pieces and place evenly in eggs and tap with index finger until they are under the eggs.   Don't close the omlet maker. Microwave for 90 seconds. There will be a little swimming pool in the middle. Eat it right from the omlet maker so the pool can't escape and eat from the sides and dip into the swimming pool.

Pick and choose

Big silver tablespoon dollop of Greek nonfat yoghurt or kefir. Mix in an apple cut into bite size pieces and cut into about 9 pieces. (options: add peas, peanuts, raisins) Mix it all together and enjoy. Could put favorite dressing.

Scottburger

Just 6% fat ground beef, Mrs. Dash no salt. Cook to desired doneness. If cheese, use Swiss.

You ate what???

!/4 cooked spaghetti squash. Top with ½ Pure Protein bar, cut into small pieces and microwave for 1minute 45 seconds.

Family Photos 1943 – Present

I was the first born. Februaru 11, 1943

My claim to fame: cover of Argus Cameras Magazine.

Merry Christmas

Ginny, Bete, Gail & Denni

Then it was Denny and me, June 6, 1948

Denny and me. Mom had a cottage before she
and Dad were married and we spent lots of time
out there in the summers.

And then came Scott, August 29, 1950

Holiday Greetings

The Petersons

A few of our Christmas cards over the years.
The folks always had a new, clever way to stage
the photos.

MERRY
CHRISTMAS

The Petersons

The Petersons

Merry Christmas

Peterson

HELLO, MERRY CHRISTMAS

THE PETERSONS

Greetings *From Our House to Your House...*

Petersons

Then school pictures took over so here are one set
of ours from I think around the same time.

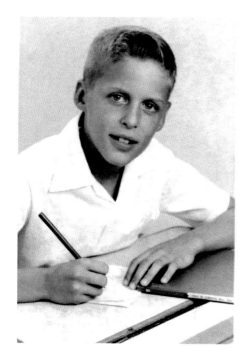

1956-57   LYNDON

Our back yard on Sanford Place, I think.
And then came color!

I don't have any pictures once I went away to college. I met my husband, Jordan, in 1975 in Hawaii where I moved after I graduated and here are a couple of photos from our wedding in Maui.

July 8, 1979, Napili Bay, Maui

We were so happy that Mom and Dad flew out and Mom was my matron of honor.

Dad walked me down the "aisle" while Mom looks on.

Group photo of Jordan's parents, his brother, and us.

1981 Scott has never really stopped playing golf.

1983 The whole family with our six month old son.
The folks sure loved us all!

UM shirt Uncles Denny & Scott gave Thumper.

Around 1986, Jordan in the background

1988 UM Museum of Natural History

Backyard on Roundtree

1988 the folks' favorite pasttime

1989 Kensington Park

Golf instruction 1990

1990 we celebrated all our birthdays at once.

1991

1992

1993 I wanted Thumper to see snow while his grandparents were alive so we spontaneously went.

Lucky I did go then. Dad passed away August 25 that year.
We went for the service but took no pictures of the family.

1996

1999

2001

2002 At the track

With Cousin Carolyn, Thumper and me. Mom and my
brothers in their "56 Racing" jackets.

2003 Fishing with Jordan and Thumper

2004 My brothers brought the horse over so he
and Mom could say goodbye to each other. Mom
loved all the horses. So did Dad.

Virginia Agnus (Meyer) Peterson
July 30, 1915 - January 7, 2004

With her loved ones around her, God called home Ginny, a beloved wife, mother, grandmother, sister, and friend to be with her husband Babe. Virginia was born on July 30, 1915 to Louis and Josephine Meyer. She lived a full and caring life while growing up in Ann Arbor. Many wonderful days were spent at her cottage on Half Moon Lake with family and friends. She was employed at the University of Michigan Hospital as a switchboard supervisor and Argus Camera as a secretary. Here she met Harold (Babe) Peterson, her devoted companion, to whom she was married for 49 years. She loved travel, having visited many foreign countries, of which Ireland (visited with son Scott) was her favorite. She also enjoyed gardening, home-making, walking with family and friends, and many joyous hours spent with grandchildren. In 1993, she founded Five Six Racing which includes many Michigan Harness Standardbred Champions and the 2001 Horse of the Year, Babe's Five Six. Ginny attended Holy Spirit Roman Catholic Church, St. Andrews, and St. Thomas throughout her rewarding life. She is survived by sons, Dennis and Scott Peterson; daughters, Gail Nagasako, Susan Wellman, Jennifer Cooper, and Jada Wester; son-in-law, Jordan Nagasako; and grandchildren, Thumper Nagasako, Michelle, Kathryn, and Brian Wellman, Nicole Cooper, and Alexa and Jordan Wester. She is also survived by many aunts, nieces, nephews and longtime friends. All were loved in the deepest way. A memorial service to celebrate Ginny's life (was) held Saturday, January 17th, 2004 at 1 p.m. at the Muehlig Chapel. The burial service (followed) at Forest Hills Cemetery.

2005 at the farm with Thumper and Julia,

Geralyn's daughter.

2005 Detroit

2007 At the stables above with Jeff, Thumper's older brother.

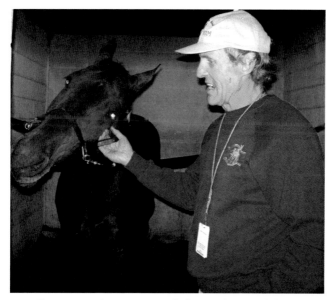

Scott at the same visit to the stables.

2007 Dinner with the Meyer cousins.

2008 Charlevoix with Geralyn, her daughter, Julia
and her sister and with our cousin, Carolyn

2008 Scott and Jordan canoeing Huron River

with Geralyn's son, Jacob.

2010 Scott, Thumper and me with Scott's Corvette

2011 Another visit to the horses.

2014 Thumper with us and his uncles

2015 Scott came to visit us in Maui.
This is along the Road to Hāna.

2017 With Scott's pride and joy!

2018, January, our big trip was an Alaskan Cruise, and in 2019, the Doskoch and Silver families visited us. Molly, Jeff, Thumper, Geralyn, John, Julia.

And I took a very short trip to Charlevoix to visit winter. Here snowshoing at Fisherman's Island with Geralyn. I also went to the West Coast to see my goddaughters and their families. And we made it to Ypsi in October but no pictures with my brothers. And then the Pandemic....

2023 the boys in Scott's car.

2024 all of us still looking good!!!

Made in the USA
Las Vegas, NV
05 December 2024

13440140R00029